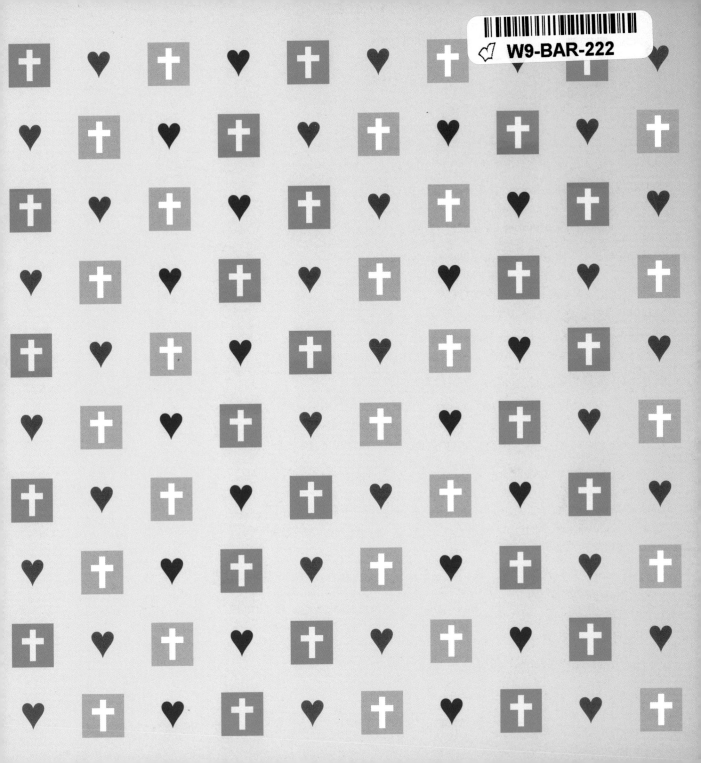

Nihil obstat: Rev. Robert A. Pesarchick, STD
                   Censor librorum
                   September 24, 2021

Imprimatur: + Most Reverend Nelson J. Perez, DD
                   Archbishop of Philadelphia
                   September 29, 2021

Ascension
PO Box 1990
West Chester, PA 19380
1-800-376-0520
ascensionpress.com

Design: Rosemary Strohm

Printed in the United States of America
ISBN 978-1-954881-05-1

Pray and Think Imaginative ROSARY BOOK

Written and Illustrated by CANDACE CAMLING

ASCENSION Kids

West Chester, Pennsylvania

Introduction

Praying the Rosary is a wonderful way to get closer to Jesus and our Mother in heaven, Mary. This book will show you how to use a special set of beads called a "rosary" (with a little "r") to pray a special set of prayers called "the Rosary" (with a big "R").

As you pray the prayers in order and make your way around your rosary, you will hold each bead between your finger and thumb. As you move from bead to bead, you will meditate (quietly think) on the mysteries. You can meditate by simply looking at the pictures in this book as you say the prayer. Asking a grown-up to go through the book with you may be helpful.

The Rosary

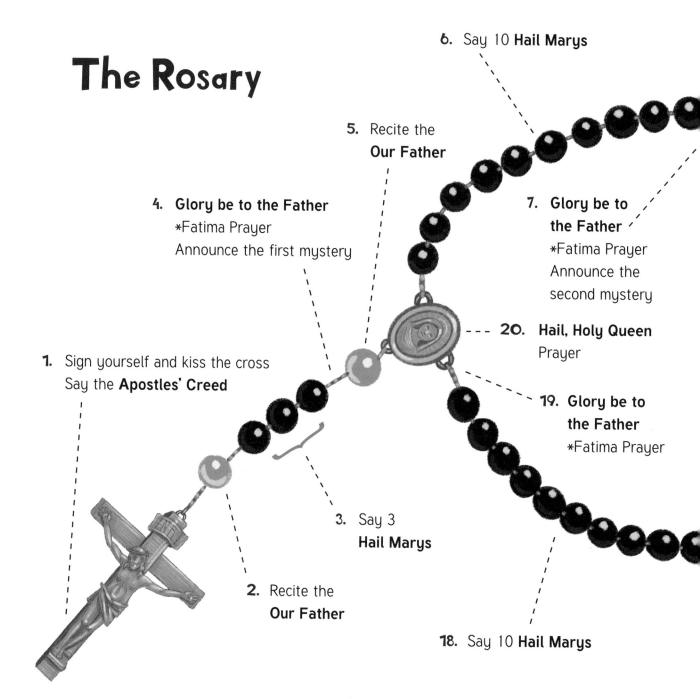

6. Say 10 **Hail Marys**

5. Recite the **Our Father**

4. **Glory be to the Father**
   *Fatima Prayer
   Announce the first mystery

7. **Glory be to the Father**
   *Fatima Prayer
   Announce the second mystery

1. Sign yourself and kiss the cross
   Say the **Apostles' Creed**

20. **Hail, Holy Queen** Prayer

19. **Glory be to the Father**
    *Fatima Prayer

3. Say 3 **Hail Marys**

2. Recite the **Our Father**

18. Say 10 **Hail Marys**

2

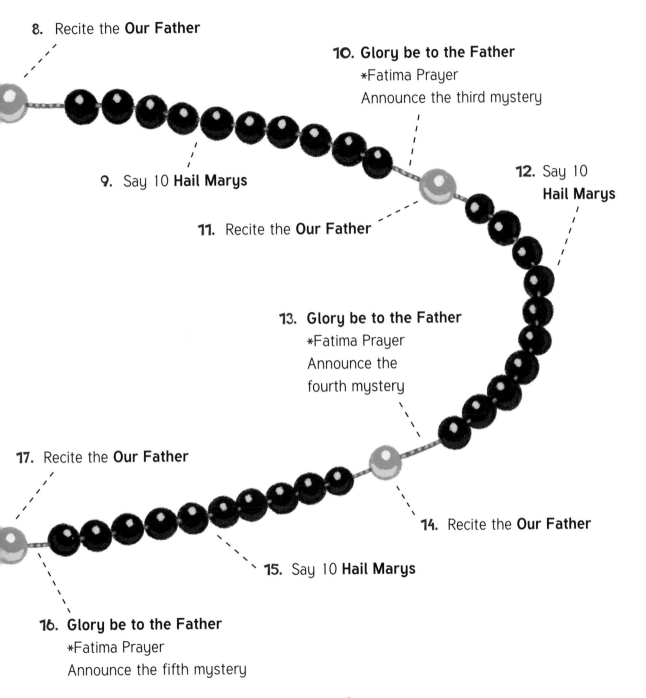

8. Recite the **Our Father**

9. Say 10 **Hail Marys**

10. Glory be to the Father
*Fatima Prayer
Announce the third mystery

11. Recite the **Our Father**

12. Say 10 **Hail Marys**

13. Glory be to the Father
*Fatima Prayer
Announce the
fourth mystery

14. Recite the **Our Father**

15. Say 10 **Hail Marys**

16. Glory be to the Father
*Fatima Prayer
Announce the fifth mystery

17. Recite the **Our Father**

Begin the Rosary Prayer

SIGN YOURSELF ...

1. In the name of the Father,

2. ... and of the Son,

3. ... and of the Holy

4. Spirit.

5. Amen.

Kiss the Cross

Say the Apostles' Creed

I believe in God,
the Father almighty,
Creator of heaven and earth,
and in Jesus Christ,
his only Son, our Lord,
who was conceived by the Holy Spirit,
born of the Virgin Mary,
suffered under Pontius Pilate,
was crucified, died and was buried;
he descended to hell;
on the third day he rose again from the dead;
he ascended into heaven,
and is seated at the right hand of God the Father almighty;
from there he will come to judge the living and the dead.
I believe in the Holy Spirit, the holy catholic Church,
the communion of saints, the forgiveness of sins,
the resurrection of the body, and life everlasting.
Amen.

How many apostles were there?

Count them to find out.

Say 1 Our Father

Our Father, who art in heaven,
hallowed be thy name;
thy kingdom come, thy will be done,
on earth as it is in heaven.
Give us this day our daily bread,
and forgive us our trespasses as
we forgive those who trespass against us;
and lead us not into temptation,
but deliver us from evil.
Amen.

Can you find all the **Our Father** prayer beads on this page? If you have a rosary in your hands, use this drawing to help you find the **Our Father** beads.

What do you notice about the **Our Father** beads? Are they in groups? Are they alone? Why do you think that might be?

Say 3 Hail Marys

Hail Mary, full of grace, the Lord is with thee.
Blessed art thou among women, and blessed is the fruit of thy womb, Jesus.
Holy Mary, Mother of God, pray for us sinners, now and at the hour of our death.
Amen.

Say 1 Glory Be

Use your finger to trace the triangle between Father, Son, and Holy Spirit. This is the **Trinity**, which means three.

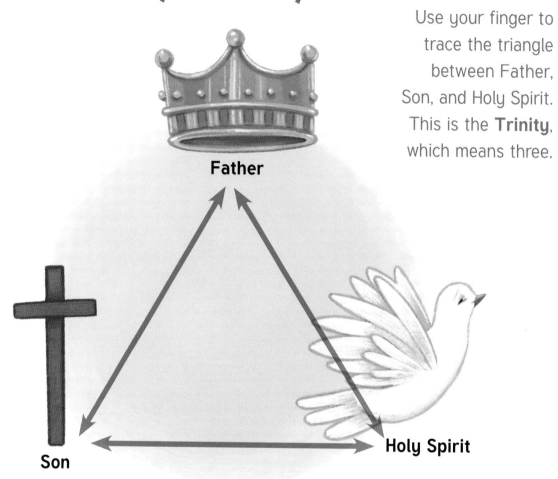

Father

Son

Holy Spirit

Glory be to the Father, and to the Son, and to the Holy Spirit, as it was in the beginning, is now, and ever shall be, world without end. Amen.

Say 1 Fatima Prayer

Mary miraculously appeared to three children. Children just like you!

While talking to the children, she asked them—and all of us—to pray the prayer below. How would you feel if Mary appeared to you?

O my Jesus, forgive us our sins, save us from the fires of hell, and lead all souls to heaven, especially those in most need of thy mercy.

Which set of mysteries will you pray today?

Each day we pray a set of mysteries, which are important moments in the life of Jesus. Look at the chart to find out which set of mysteries to pray.

Day of the week		Mystery of the Rosary
SUNDAY	→	GLORIOUS
MONDAY	→	JOYFUL
TUESDAY	→	SORROWFUL
WEDNESDAY	→	GLORIOUS
THURSDAY	→	LIGHT
FRIDAY	→	SORROWFUL
SATURDAY	→	JOYFUL

Joyful Mysteries

Announce the first Joyful Mystery:

The Annunciation

Say 1 **Our Father**

Say 10 **Hail Marys**

Say 1 **Glory Be**

Say 1 **Fatima Prayer**

The Annunciation

Gabriel the angel tells Mary she will conceive Jesus through the Holy Spirit.
Look at the picture of the mystery. Then turn the page to help you meditate on the mystery.

This is a dove. A dove is a symbol of the Holy Spirit. Trace the rays of light from the dove to Mary. Do you know why there is a dove in the picture? It is because the Holy Spirit was with Mary.

Touch the flower in the angel Gabriel's hand. Do you know what kind of flower it is? It is a lily. Lilies are pure and beautiful. Mary was pure and beautiful like a lily.

Mary said yes to God. Imagine sitting next to Mary. What would you like to ask her about? What do you think she would say to you?

Joyful Mysteries

Announce the second Joyful Mystery:

The Visitation

Say 1 **Our Father**

Say 10 **Hail Marys**

Say 1 **Glory Be**

Say 1 **Fatima Prayer**

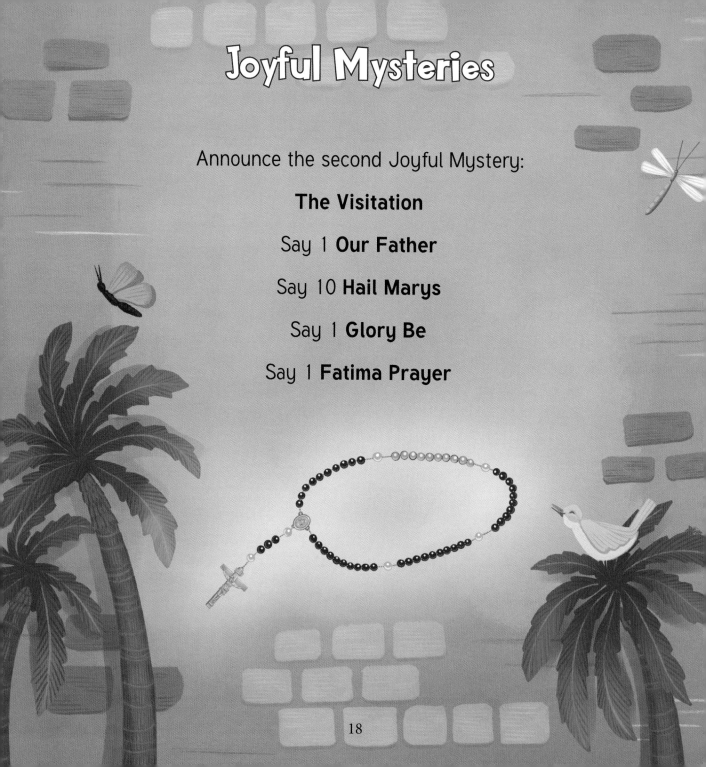

The Visitation

Mary and her cousin Elizabeth greet each other. John the Baptist leaps in Elizabeth's womb.
Look at the picture of the mystery. Then turn the page to help you meditate on the mystery.

Touch Elizabeth's gray hair. Do you know why her pregnancy was a miracle? It is because she was so old, and God helped her to have a child.

Do you see that Elizabeth is going to have a baby? Do you know who that baby is? It is John the Baptist, Jesus' cousin, who will later baptize him.

Look at Mary's mouth. When Mary meets Elizabeth, she praises God. Her words are called the Magnificat. You can praise God right now.

Joyful Mysteries

Announce the third Joyful Mystery:

The Nativity

Say 1 **Our Father**

Say 10 **Hail Marys**

Say 1 **Glory Be**

Say 1 **Fatima Prayer**

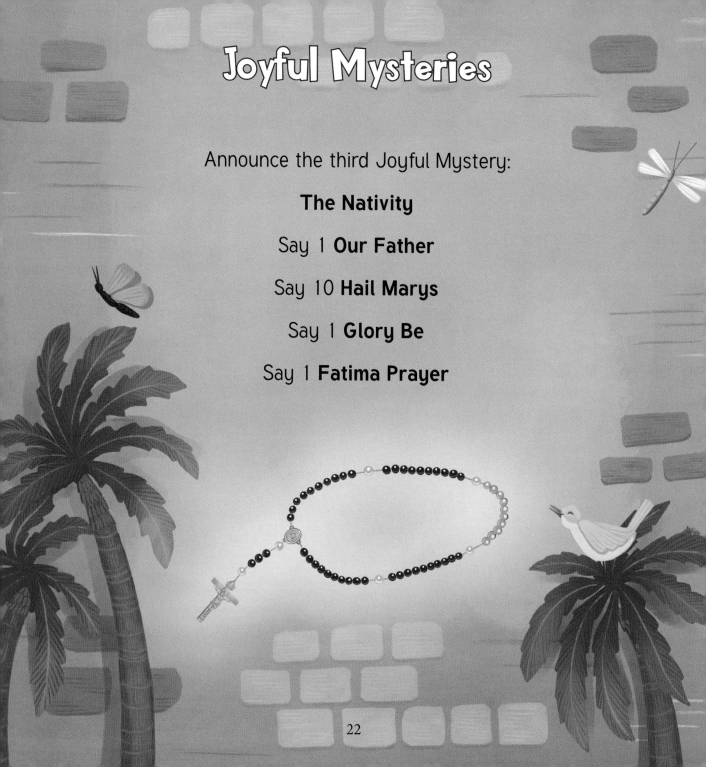

The Nativity

Jesus is born in a humble stable.

Look at the picture of the mystery. Then turn the page to help you meditate on the mystery.

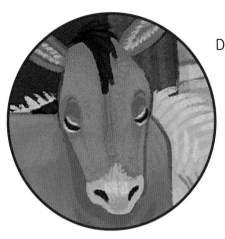

Do you see the donkey? It is a symbol for Jesus' humble beginnings in a stable.

Touch the lamb. Jesus is the Lamb of God.

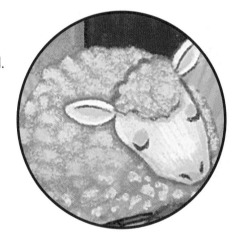

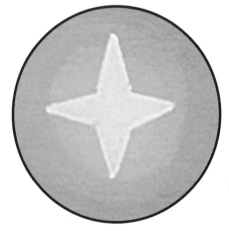

Point to the star. Do you know who used the star as a guide? It was the three wise men.

Joyful Mysteries

Announce the fourth Joyful Mystery:

The Presentation in the Temple

Say 1 **Our Father**

Say 10 **Hail Marys**

Say 1 **Glory Be**

Say 1 **Fatima Prayer**

The Presentation in the Temple

Jesus is brought to the Temple and "redeemed" by Joseph's offering of two young pigeons.
Meditate on the image of the mystery.

Touch the pigeons. They represent a sacrifice. A sacrifice is giving something up. Have you ever had to sacrifice something?

Look at Mary's hands. She is offering Jesus like she will do again at the Cross.

Simeon is holding Jesus. He is holding salvation.

Joyful Mysteries

Announce the fifth Joyful Mystery:

The Finding in the Temple

Say 1 **Our Father**

Say 10 **Hail Marys**

Say 1 **Glory Be**

Say 1 **Fatima Prayer**

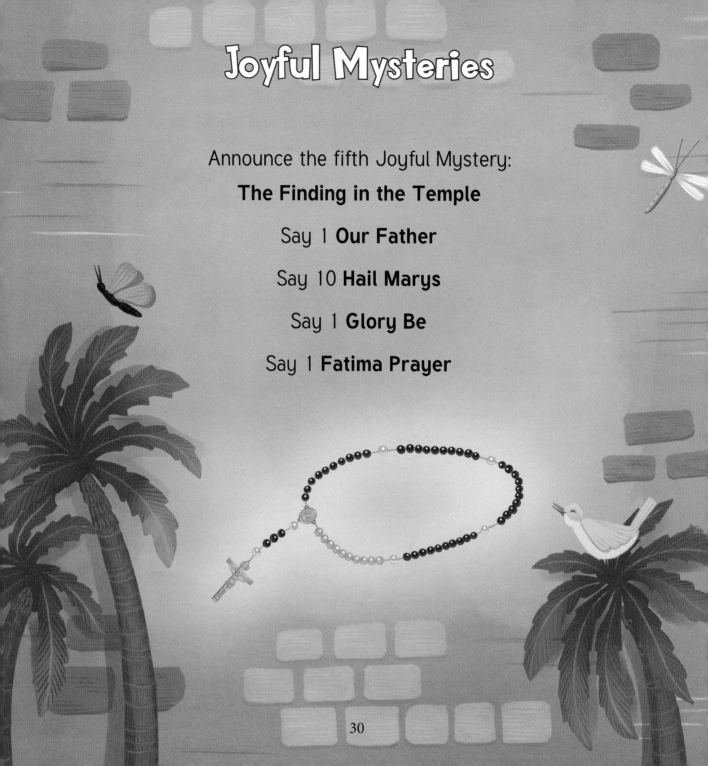

The Finding in the Temple

Instead of following a caravan with his mother and father,
Jesus makes his way to the Temple to "be about his Father's business."

Do you see the men surrounding Jesus? Do you know who they are? They are men who studied God's Word.

See Jesus' face. At your age now, how do you respond to God's will?

Touch the scroll. Jesus fulfills the Law.

Mysteries of Light

Announce the first Mystery of Light:

Jesus' Baptism in the Jordan River

Say 1 **Our Father**

Say 10 **Hail Marys**

Say 1 **Glory Be**

Say 1 **Fatima Prayer**

Jesus' Baptism in the Jordan River

Jesus is baptized by John the Baptist. The Holy Spirit descends upon Jesus.
Meditate on the image of the mystery.

Do you see the dove? It is a symbol for the Holy Spirit coming upon Jesus.

Why is Jesus in the water? He is about to be baptized. Have you ever seen someone be baptized?

Mysteries of Light

Announce the second Mystery of Light:

Jesus' Self-Manifestation at the Wedding at Cana

Say 1 **Our Father**

Say 10 **Hail Marys**

Say 1 **Glory Be**

Say 1 **Fatima Prayer**

Jesus' Self-Manifestation at the Wedding at Cana

Jesus changes water into wine at a wedding in Cana.
Meditate on the image of the mystery.

Touch the empty jar. Do you know what Jesus does for this jar? He fills it, like he fills us.

Touch Mary's hand. She is close to Jesus, and she intercedes for us.

See the servant's face. Sometimes God surprises us, but we still must obey.

Mysteries of Light

Announce the third Mystery of Light:

Jesus' Proclamation of the Kingdom of God

Say 1 **Our Father**

Say 10 **Hail Marys**

Say 1 **Glory Be**

Say 1 **Fatima Prayer**

Jesus' Proclamation of the Kingdom of God

Jesus preaches the truth to all who will listen.
Meditate on the image of the mystery.

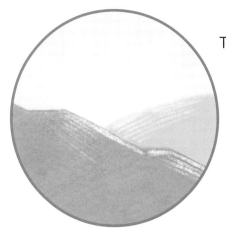

Touch the mountain. In the Sermon on the Mount, Jesus tells us how to live, like God told us long ago at Mount Sinai.

You are a unique person. How do you respond to God?

These are the beatitudes Jesus taught in the Sermon on the Mount:

Blessed are the poor in spirit,
for theirs is the kingdom of heaven.

Blessed are those who mourn,
for they shall be comforted.

Blessed are the meek,
for they shall inherit the earth.

Blessed are those who hunger and thirst
for righteousness,
for they shall be satisfied.

Blessed are the merciful,
for they shall obtain mercy.

Blessed are the pure in heart,
for they shall see God.

Blessed are the peacemakers,
for they shall be called sons of God.

Blessed are those who are persecuted
for righteousness' sake,
for theirs is the kingdom of heaven.

Blessed are you when men revile you
and persecute you and utter all kinds of
evil against you falsely on my account.
Rejoice and be glad, for your reward is
great in heaven, for so men persecuted
the prophets who were before you.

(Matthew 5:3-12)

Mysteries of Light

Announce the fourth Mystery of Light:

Jesus' Transfiguration

Say 1 **Our Father**

Say 10 **Hail Marys**

Say 1 **Glory Be**

Say 1 **Fatima Prayer**

Jesus' Transfiguration

Jesus becomes glowing white on a mountain, appearing to his disciples alongside Moses and Elijah. Meditate on the image of the mystery.

Touch Jesus' clothing. If you saw Jesus glowing, how would you respond?

Who is holding the tablets on Jesus' side? It is Moses, and the tablets contain the Ten Commandments.

Who is the other man on Jesus' other side? It is Elijah. He was a prophet.

Mysteries of Light

Announce the fifth Mystery of Light:

Jesus' Institution of the Holy Eucharist

Say 1 **Our Father**

Say 10 **Hail Marys**

Say 1 **Glory Be**

Say 1 **Fatima Prayer**

Jesus' Institution of the Holy Eucharist

Jesus teaches his disciples to receive his Body and Blood.
Meditate on the image of the mystery.

What do you see in front of Jesus? It looks like bread and wine, but it is his Body and Blood.

See Jesus' face. We can't see his face at Mass, but Jesus is present in the Eucharist.

Jesus is surrounded by his apostles. Do you think they are eager to receive the Eucharist? Are you eager to receive Jesus in the Eucharist?

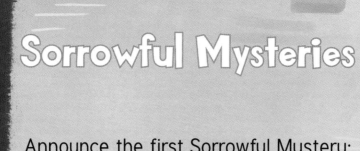

Sorrowful Mysteries

Announce the first Sorrowful Mystery:

The Agony in the Garden

Say 1 **Our Father**

Say 10 **Hail Marys**

Say 1 **Glory Be**

Say 1 **Fatima Prayer**

The Agony in the Garden

Jesus prays in a garden. He sweats blood while the disciples sleep.
Meditate on the image of the mystery.

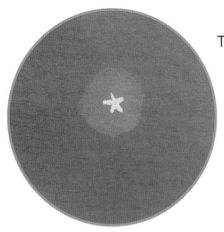

Touch the sky. Do you think Jesus felt deep loneliness in the garden?

Jesus sweats blood. Why do you think he did that?

Even in agony, Jesus prays and accepts God's will.

Sorrowful Mysteries

Announce the second Sorrowful Mystery:

The Scourging

Say 1 **Our Father**

Say 10 **Hail Marys**

Say 1 **Glory Be**

Say 1 **Fatima Prayer**

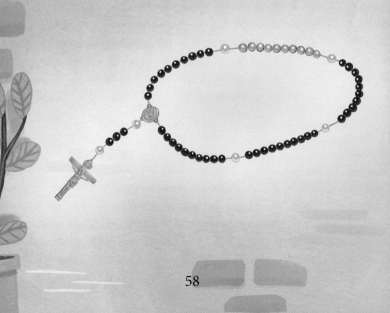

The Scourging

Roman soldiers badly beat and whip Jesus' body.
Meditate on the image of the mystery.

Do you see Jesus' face? He accepts suffering for us.

Just like the scourge,
our sins hurt Jesus.

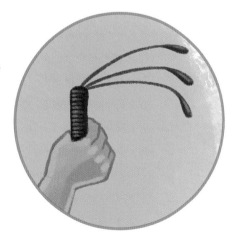

Sorrowful Mysteries

Announce the third Sorrowful Mystery:

The Crowning with Thorns

Say 1 **Our Father**

Say 10 **Hail Marys**

Say 1 **Glory Be**

Say 1 **Fatima Prayer**

The Crowning with Thorns

Roman soldiers place a crown of thorns upon Jesus' head.
Meditate on the image of the mystery.

Touch Jesus' crown of thorns.
He accepts ridicule and pain
with courage.

Jesus' tears are part of
his suffering for us.

Sorrowful Mysteries

Announce the fourth Sorrowful Mystery:

The Carrying of the Cross

Say 1 **Our Father**

Say 10 **Hail Marys**

Say 1 **Glory Be**

Say 1 **Fatima Prayer**

The Carrying of the Cross

Jesus carries his own cross, stumbling along the way.
Meditate on the image of the mystery.

Jesus willingly carries the Cross. What are you willing to do for God?

Do you think the Cross is heavy? Jesus carries it patiently.

We are called to carry our own crosses even when it doesn't seem to make sense. Carrying a cross is a way of dealing with something hard in your own life.

Sorrowful Mysteries

Announce the fifth Sorrowful Mystery:

The Crucifixion

Say 1 **Our Father**

Say 10 **Hail Marys**

Say 1 **Glory Be**

Say 1 **Fatima Prayer**

The Crucifixion

Jesus is crucified and dies on the Cross.
Meditate on the image of the mystery.

Trace the letters INRI. What do they mean? They mean "Jesus of Nazareth, King of the Jews."

Touch the nail wounds on Jesus' hands and feet. They show his love for us.

As Jesus died on the Cross, he saved the whole world.

Glorious Mysteries

Announce the first Glorious Mystery:

The Resurrection

Say 1 **Our Father**

Say 10 **Hail Marys**

Say 1 **Glory Be**

Say 1 **Fatima Prayer**

The Resurrection

Jesus is risen from the dead. He is alive!
Meditate on the image of the mystery.

Touch the rock. What did the women find when they rolled away the rock? They found an empty tomb.

Do you know who this is? It is Mary Magdalene, and she is going to spread the good news of Jesus' resurrection.

Jesus calls the women's names. Just like he calls our names.

Glorious Mysteries

Announce the second Glorious Mystery:

The Ascension

Say 1 **Our Father**

Say 10 **Hail Marys**

Say 1 **Glory Be**

Say 1 **Fatima Prayer**

The Ascension

Jesus ascends to heaven.
Meditate on the image of the mystery.

Do the hands of Jesus look like your priest's hands at Mass sometimes?

Look at Jesus' feet. They still have the marks of crucifixion.

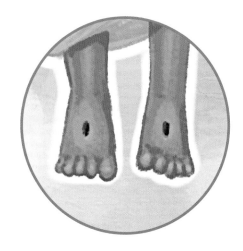

Just like he went up to heaven, Jesus will return to earth.

Glorious Mysteries

Announce the third Glorious Mystery:

The Descent of the Holy Spirit

Say 1 **Our Father**

Say 10 **Hail Marys**

Say 1 **Glory Be**

Say 1 **Fatima Prayer**

The Descent of the Holy Spirit

The Holy Spirit comes upon those who will teach, comfort, and help the early Church.
Meditate on the image of the mystery.

Touch the flame. The apostles received the Holy Spirit and were inspired to teach others about God's Word. How does Jesus' life inspire you?

Touch the dove. The Holy Spirit is often shown as a dove flying.

Glorious Mysteries

Announce the fourth Glorious Mystery:

The Assumption

Say 1 **Our Father**

Say 10 **Hail Marys**

Say 1 **Glory Be**

Say 1 **Fatima Prayer**

The Assumption

Mary is taken to heaven, body and soul.
Meditate on the image of the mystery.

What do you think heaven is like?

Mary was assumed to heaven body and soul.
That means all of her went to heaven.

Touch Mary's face. How happy do you
think Mary is right now?

Glorious Mysteries

Announce the fifth Glorious Mystery:

The Coronation

Say 1 **Our Father**

Say 10 **Hail Marys**

Say 1 **Glory Be**

Say 1 **Fatima Prayer**

The Coronation

Mary is crowned Queen of heaven and earth.
Meditate on the image of the mystery.

Touch Mary's crown. Why do you think we pray to her? It is because she is Queen of heaven and intercedes for us. That means she acts on our behalf when we pray to her.

Who is crowning Mary as Queen of heaven? It is her son, the Son of God, Jesus.

Hail, Holy Queen

Hail, Holy Queen, Mother of mercy, our life, our sweetness, and our hope. To thee do we cry, poor banished children of Eve; to thee do we send up our sighs, mourning and weeping in this valley of tears. Turn, then, most gracious advocate, thine eyes of mercy toward us, and after this, our exile, show unto us the blessed fruit of thy womb, Jesus. O clement, O loving, O sweet Virgin Mary.

Congratulations!

Now that you know how to pray the Rosary,
you can join the millions of people around the world
who pray this special set of prayers every day.
Every moment someone, somewhere, is praying the Rosary.
Won't you pray with them?